KUNAL KAPUR
IN THE
KITCHEN
FAMILY MEALS

Foreword
GAGGAN ANAND

Om Books International

First published in 2021 by

Om Books International

Corporate & Editorial Office
A-12, Sector 64, Noida 201 301
Uttar Pradesh, India
Phone: +91 120 477 4100
Email: editorial@ombooks.com
Website: www.ombooksinternational.com

Sales Office
107, Ansari Road, Darya Ganj, New Delhi 110 002, India
Phone: +91 11 4000 9000
Email: sales@ombooks.com
Website: www.ombooks.com

ISBN: 9789352766178

Printed in India

10 9 8 7 6 5 4 3 2 1

Contents

Drinks   Veg   Non-Veg

It was the summer of 2000 when I first met Kunal. I have vivid memories of that day when the best aspiring chefs of the country—the so-called 'Taj ke Damad'—were all gathered in a room at the Taj Palace Hotel in Delhi. We were fresh recruits from our respective colleges, who had joined as kitchen management trainees with the Taj group. Prompt and an extrovert, Kunal immediately befriended me. It's been almost 20 years and our friendship has stood the test of time.

During our days at the Taj, I realised Kunal was extremely passionate about Indian cuisine. He always wanted to explore and master the little techniques of cooking a perfect Indian dish. Slowly and steadily, Kunal grew to be an excellent learner; his extensive research on the lost and hidden culinary treasures of India is admirable.

In 2007, when I moved to Bangkok, we lost touch. A few years later, when I saw him as the judge of the TV series MasterChef India, I said, "I know this guy, he's our Kunal". I still remember how he taught the contestants on the show the secret to cooking authentic biryani. The way he supported and evaluated the finalists was commendable.

Two decades ago, my friend set out on a journey with a mission. After all the efforts he put in and the time he invested to polish his already extraordinary work in the kitchen, Chef Kunal Kapur is a name to reckon with. He is a true showman, a foodie, an adventurer, a charmer, and of course, a committed chef.

Today, he has risen to be the poster boy celebrity chef who has added a whole new dimension to the culinary industry in India. I wish him all the best and congratulate him on yet another milestone—
Kunal Kapur in the Kitchen.

—Gaggan Anand
Renowned Indian chef and erstwhile owner of the progressive Indian 2-Michelin star restaurant Gaggan, Bangkok, Thailand—ranked No. 4 in the world in 2019 & No. 1 in Asia for the fourth consecutive time in the World's 50 Best Restaurants list.

Bonding Over Food

I grew up in a humble Punjabi joint family in Delhi. After Partition, my grandparents from Lahore started a new life with three children in Delhi. Though sustaining a family seemed tough, their resilience and tenacity were admirable. Both worked hard and left no stone unturned in the well-being of their children. Interestingly, they always cooked together. Since childhood, I have watched men, especially my grandfather, father and uncle donning the chef's hat in the kitchen. My grandfather loved to experiment in the kitchen and every now and then, he would come up with his own specialties and gastronomic delights.

As a chef, I try to imbibe his subtleties and little techniques when I am cooking. Men taking charge of the kitchen was not something that I considered peculiar. In fact, I am proud to confess that my first lessons in cooking were taught by them.

My grandfather was a thorough gentleman. He had studied in a British school and was a man of principles and discipline. There were two ground rules set by him: first, food would be served at the dining table and only at the dining table, and second, everybody must eat together. Children of the house would take turns to set and clean the table. When I look back, I realise the true meaning and purpose of this ritual—creating strong bonds—that I hold close to my heart even today. Some of the most engaging conversations took place at the dining table. Each and every member of the family connected over food.

Food is food, but a good meal is the route to bring family and friends together. You don't have to wait for a special day, all you need to do is whip up a delicious meal for your dear ones and make them feel loved.

This book comprising 15 choicest meals is not only a nostalgia trip for a boy from a big Punjabi family, but also a reminder of what all of us can do best—share a meal together. These popular yet unique meals are conversation starters, fun and easy-to-cook and of course, scrumptious. Add your own variation to these meals and promise yourself a memorable dining experience.

Happy cooking from *Kunal Kapur in the Kitchen*!

Meal 01

Serves

Strawberry & Ginger Sangria

•

Indian Pomelo Salad

•

Seekh Kebab with Onion Tamarind Chutney

•

Tomato & Rosemary Pulao

•

Mango Lassi Ice Cream

strawberry & Ginger Sangria

INGREDIENTS

Strawberry	**6 nos.**
Rosemary	**2 sprigs**
Honey	**1 tbsp**
White wine (dry)	**200 ml**
Ginger ale	**100 ml**

NOTES

For this recipe, make sure both ginger ale and white wine are chilled.

METHOD

- In a cocktail shaker, add 4 fresh strawberries and 1 rosemary sprig. Using a muddler, squash the ingredients.

- Pour honey and 100 ml white wine to the above mix. Close the cocktail shaker and shake it vigorously.

- Strain and divide into 2 glasses equally. Top up with the remaining wine followed by chilled ginger ale.

- Before serving, garnish with a strawberry and a sprig of rosemary each.

Indian Pomelo Salad

Cumin seeds	**2 tsp**
Pomelo	**1 no.** (small) (peeled & segments removed)
Black salt	**1/2 tsp**
Salt	**a pinch**
Black pepper	**a pinch**
Sugar	**2 tbsp** (powdered)
Lemon	**1 no.**
Mint leaves	**1 cup**

- In a preheated pan, add cumin seeds and lightly roast till the colour changes to a darker shade. Remove and lightly crush the seeds.

- In a separate bowl, place the pomelo. Add black salt, salt, black pepper, roasted cumin and sugar.

- Squeeze lemon and add mint leaves to the mix.

- Toss and serve chilled.

Seekh Kebab with Onion Tamarind Chutney

INGREDIENTS

Lamb (fatty)	**250 gm** (minced)
Garlic	**3 cloves**
Ginger	**1 small knob**
Coriander	**few sprigs**
Mint leaves	**fistful**
Green chilli	**1/2 no.**
Cumin	**2 tsp**
Cheese	**50 gm**
	(semi-hard or processed)
Kashmiri chilli powder	**2 tsp**
Salt	**1 tsp**
Oil	**1 tbsp**
Butter	**for basting**
Chaat masala	**a generous pinch** (optional)

FOR THE CHUTNEY

Onion	**1/2 cup** (chopped)
Tamarind pulp	**1/4 cup**
Ginger	**2 tsp** (chopped)
Green chilli	**1 no.** (finely chopped)
Coriander	**few sprigs** (chopped)
Salt	**to taste**
Black salt	**1/2 tsp**
Water	**a dash**

METHOD

- In a blender, add minced lamb and all the listed ingredients except oil, butter and chaat masala. Blend for about a minute till all the ingredients are finely ground.

- Wet your hands with water. Take a small portion of the minced lamb and make small cylinders of about 2" long and 1/2" wide.

- Take a pan and lightly grease the surface with oil. Heat the pan on medium flame.

- Place the seekh kebabs on the medium-hot pan and cook them on all sides for 12-15 minutes.

- Remove and baste with butter. Sprinkle chaat masala over the seekh kebabs.

- For the chutney, mix all the ingredients and gently crush the onions using your hands. Allow to rest for 5 minutes.

- Stir and serve cold with the piping hot seekh kebabs.

Tomato & Rosemary Pulao

INGREDIENTS

Oil	**4 tbsp**
Onion	**1 no.** (small) (peeled & roughly chopped)
Garlic	**5 cloves** (crushed & chopped)
Rosemary	**4 sprigs**
Green chilli	**1 no.** (slit)
Tomato	**5 nos.** (chopped)
Salt	**1 tsp**
Pepper	**1/2 tsp**
Water	**2 cups**
Basmati rice	**1 cup** (soaked for 30 minutes)

METHOD

- In a pan, heat oil and add onions and garlic. Sauté for 2-3 minutes on medium flame.

- Add rosemary sprigs and sauté again.

- Add green chilli and tomatoes. Cook the tomatoes for 5 minutes.

- Add salt, pepper and water. Bring this mix to a boil.

- Strain the excess water from the soaked rice and add the rice to the pan. Cook on high flame and bring to a boil.

- Lower the flame and cook (covered) till all the water is absorbed. Turn off the flame and let the rice rest for 5 minutes.

- Using a fork, fluff up the rice and serve hot.

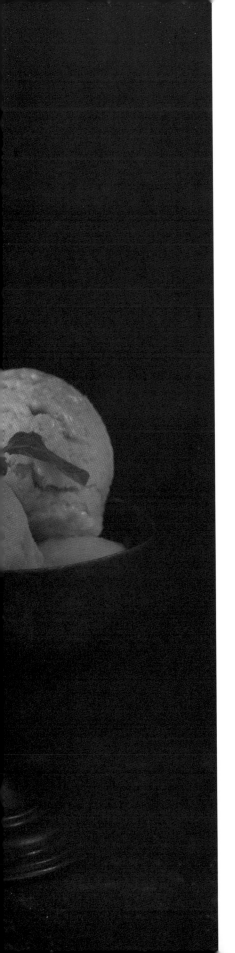

Mango Lassi Ice Cream

INGREDIENTS

Mango	**2 nos.** (large) (peeled & pulp removed)
Curd	**1 cup** (thick)
Sugar	**3 tbsp**

METHOD

- In a blender, add mangoes, curd and sugar. Blend into a smooth purée.

- Pour the purée into a tub or ice cream moulds. Freeze these for about 2 hours and remove. Using a whisk, stir so that there are no or very few ice crystals.

- Keep the moulds in the deep freezer till completely frozen.

- Scoop and serve frozen.

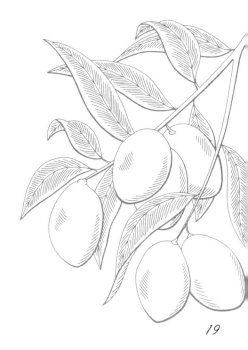

Meal 02

serves

Cherry Tomato Salad

•

Hasselback Potatoes with Aam Papad Sauce

•

Single Pot Mutton Curry

•

Ragi Roti

•

Salted Peanut Butter Caramel Kulfi

Cherry Tomato Salad

INGREDIENTS

Olive oil	**2 tbsp**
Cumin	**1 tsp**
Garlic	**2 cloves** (smashed & chopped)
Celery	**1 stick** (medium) (finely chopped)
Onion	**1 no.** (small) (peeled & roughly sliced)
Cherry tomato	**2 cups** (cut into two)
Balsamic vinegar	**3 tbsp**
Salt	**to taste**
Pepper	**to taste**
Sugar	**2 tsp**
Dill leaves	**handful** (finely chopped)

METHOD

- Heat a pan and add olive oil.

- Add cumin and once it crackles, add garlic, celery and onions. Sauté for a minute.

- Add cherry tomatoes, vinegar, salt, pepper and sugar. Give the mix a toss on high flame for 2 minutes and remove.

- Add dill leaves to the mix.

- Toss and serve the salad warm.

Hasselback Potatoes with Aam Papad Sauce

INGREDIENTS

Potato	**4 nos.** (medium)
Butter	**2 tbsp** (softened)
Basil	**2 sprigs** (chopped)
Ginger	**1 tbsp** (chopped)
Salt	**to taste**
Pepper	**to taste**

FOR THE AAM PAPAD SAUCE

Candied mango (*aam papad*)	**200 gm** (roughly chopped)
Lemon	**1 no.**
Salt	**to taste**
Black salt	**to taste**
Cumin	**1 tsp** (roasted)
Red chilli powder	**1/2 tsp**
Water	**3 cups**

METHOD

- Slightly nip the base of the potatoes so they don't roll. Now, slit the potatoes till the middle. Make about 12-15 such slits.

- In a bowl, add butter, basil, ginger, salt and pepper. Smear this flavoured butter on and inside the slits of the potatoes. Place these on a roasting tray and cook in a preheated oven at 180 degrees for about 35 minutes or till the potatoes are done.

- In a pan, add all the ingredients for the sauce and cook on low heat till aam papad dissolves completely. Once it thickens enough to coat a spoon, remove.

- Pour the aam papad sauce on a serving plate and arrange the potatoes over it.

- Serve hot or warm.

Single Pot Mutton Curry

INGREDIENTS

Mutton	**400 gm** (cleaned)
Salt	**to taste**
Black salt	**2 tsp**
Black pepper	**1 tbsp** (pounded)
Turmeric	**2 tsp**
Chilli powder	**2 tsp**
Cumin powder	**1 tbsp**
Coriander seeds	**2 tbsp** (pounded)
Coriander powder	**2 tbsp**
Fenugreek leaves powder (*methi*)	**1 tsp**
Onion	**2 cups** (sliced)
Fried onion	**2 cups**
Curd	**2 cups** (whisked)
Green chilli	**2 nos.** (slit)
Oil	**2/3 cup**
Ginger paste	**2 tbsp**
Garlic paste	**2 tbsp**
Water	**as required**
Coriander stem	**handful** (roughly chopped)

METHOD

- Marinate the mutton with salt, black salt, black pepper, turmeric, chilli powder, cumin powder, coriander seeds, coriander powder, fenugreek leaves powder, onions, fried onions, curd and green chilli. Mix well and keep aside.

- In a thick-bottom pan, heat oil and add ginger-garlic paste. Sauté for 2-3 minutes on high heat. Add marinated mutton and cook to a good boil.

- Lower the heat, cover and cook till the mutton is tender. If required, add little water or stock at regular intervals.

- Once ready, add coriander stems and stir.

- Remove and serve hot.

Ragi Roti

INGREDIENTS

Ragi flour	1 cup
Whole wheat flour	1½ cups
Salt	a pinch
Chilli powder	a pinch
Coriander leaves	handful (finely chopped)
Water	as required
Ghee	for basting

METHOD

- In a bowl, add ragi flour, 1 cup of whole wheat flour, salt, chilli powder and coriander leaves.

- Add sufficient water to make a stiff dough. Allow the dough to rest for 10 minutes.

- Divide the dough into 4 equal-sized balls. Using the remaining dry flour, roll these into thin disc-like rotis.

- Heat a pan and cook the rotis on both sides.

- Remove, smear the rotis with ghee and serve hot.

Salted Peanut Butter Caramel Kulfi

INGREDIENTS

FOR THE KULFI

Peanuts	**3 tbsp** (roasted)
Milk (full cream)	**2.5 litre**
Sugar	**50 gm**
Vanilla extract	**1 tsp**
Peanut butter	**15 gm**

FOR THE SALTED CARAMEL

Sugar	**1/2 cup**
Cream	**1/4 cup**
Butter (salted)	**40 gm**
Salt	**a pinch**

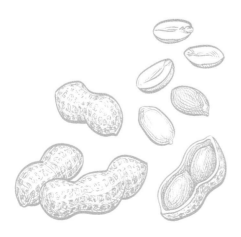

METHOD

- Gently crush the roasted peanuts, wrapped in a kitchen towel, with the help of a rolling pin.

- In a pan, add milk and bring it to a boil on slow flame, stirring continuously till it reduces to 1/3rd. Remove and add sugar and vanilla extract. Whisk thoroughly. Allow the mix to cool down completely and put it in a blender.

- Add peanut butter and blend the mix to get a smooth liquid. Pour the mix into moulds, drop some crushed peanuts and refrigerate till the mix freezes completely and becomes kulfi.

- For the salted caramel, in a separate pan, add sugar and gently heat till it caramelises to amber colour.

- Add cream and whisk well. Cook for a minute and remove from the heat.

- Add butter and sprinkle salt. Allow the mix to cool down completely.

- Remove the kulfi from the refrigerator, pour the salted caramel and serve.

Meal 03

 serves

Tempered Yoghurt Soup

•

Banana Flower Salad

•

Meat Lentil Curry

•

Garlic & Mint Parantha

•

Thandai Crème Brûlée

Tempered Yoghurt Soup

INGREDIENTS

Yoghurt	**1½ cups**
Gram flour (*besan*)	**1 tbsp**
Turmeric	**1/4 tsp**
Water	**1 cup**
Oil	**2 tbsp**
Dry red chilli	**1 no.**
Mustard seeds	**2 tsp**
Cumin	**2 tsp**
Asafoetida (*hing*)	**1/2 tsp**
Curry leaves	**1 sprig**
Onion	**1/4 no.** (small) (finely chopped)
Ginger	**a tiny piece** (chopped)
Green chilli	**1/2 no.**
Tomato	**1/2 no.** (small) (chopped)
Salt	**to taste**
Fresh coriander	**few sprigs**

METHOD

- In a bowl, add yoghurt, gram flour, turmeric and water. Whisk well and make sure there are no lumps.

- Heat a pan, add oil followed by dry red chilli.

- Cook the chilli for a few seconds and add mustard seeds and cumin. Let them pop.

- Add asafoetida and give a quick stir.

- Add curry leaves, onion, ginger and green chilli. Stir for a minute and add tomatoes. Sauté for a minute and add whisked yoghurt to the mix. On a high flame, keep whisking the mix until it reaches a boil.

- Add salt and allow the mix to simmer for 10-12 minutes or till the yoghurt acquires a thin consistency.

- Remove and serve hot. Garnish with fresh coriander sprigs and chilli oil (optional).

Banana Flower Salad

INGREDIENTS

Banana flower	**1 no.** (medium)
Water	**as required** (chilled, for soaking)
Lemon	**2 nos.**
Olive oil	**1 tbsp**
Honey	**2 tbsp**
Salt	**a generous pinch**
Pepper	**a pinch**
Sesame seeds	**1 tbsp** (toasted)
Mint leaves	**handful**
Peanuts	**1/2 cup** (toasted)

METHOD

- Wash the banana flower and peel the thick petals. Carefully remove the filament under each petal and keep aside.

- Keep the chilled water ready on the side and squeeze 1 lemon into the water.

- Now, pile up the petals and shred these into thin slices. Immediately, transfer them into the chilled water.

- In a separate bowl, add olive oil, honey, salt, pepper and sesame seeds. Whisk well. Squeeze the remaining lemon into this mix. Keep this dressing aside.

- Pull out the petals from the chilled water and shake off to drain the excess water.

- In a salad bowl, put the petals, add mint leaves, peanuts and pour the previously prepared dressing.

- Toss and serve chilled.

Meat Lentil Curry

INGREDIENTS

Oil	1/2 cup
Dry red chilli	2 nos.
Black cardamom	2 nos.
Cinnamon	1 no. (small)
Mustard seeds	1 tbsp
Onion	2 nos. (large) (finely sliced)
Mutton	400 gm (with bones)
Curry leaves	few sprigs
Ginger paste	2 tbsp
Garlic paste	2 tbsp
Green chilli	2 nos. (chopped)
Salt	to taste
Turmeric	1 tsp
Red chilli powder	2 tsp
Coriander powder	2 tbsp
Bengal gram split (*chana dal*)	1/2 cup (washed, cleaned & soaked for 1/2 hour)
Water	8 cups
Tamarind pulp	1/4 cup
Coriander leaves	for garnish

METHOD

- In a pot, heat oil and add dry red chilli, black cardamom, cinnamon and mustard seeds.

- Once the mustard seeds begin to splatter, add onions and cook till brown.

- Add mutton, curry leaves, ginger-garlic paste and green chillies. Cook the mutton for 10 minutes on medium heat.

- Add salt, turmeric, red chilli powder and coriander powder. Cook for another 5 minutes.

- Add Bengal gram and water. Cook the mutton (covered) till tender.

- Add tamarind pulp for mild acidity.

- Garnish with fresh coriander leaves.

- Serve hot.

Garlic & Mint Parantha

INGREDIENTS

Garlic	2 cloves
Green chilli	1 no.
Mint leaves	2 cups
Salt	to taste
Whole wheat flour	3 cups
Butter	50 gm
Oil/Ghee	3 tbsp

METHOD

- Using a pestle and mortar, grind garlic, green chilli and mint leaves with a pinch of salt till it becomes a paste.

- Keep aside 1/2 cup of dry flour. Make a dough using the remaining flour and add mint-garlic-chilli paste along with some water.

- Divide the dough into 4 equal balls. Allow these to rest for 5 minutes.

- Melt the butter and place it in a bowl.

- Now, roll out a ball of dough and baste it with butter on one side. On the same side, sprinkle with dry flour.

- Fold the dough into a semi-circle, baste with butter again and fold to make a triangle. Dunk the dough into the dry flour and roll out the parantha.

- On a hot griddle, cook the parantha on both sides. Apply ghee or oil to make it crisp.

- Serve hot.

Thandai Crème Brûlée

INGREDIENTS

Milk	**1 cup**
Cream	**1 cup**
Vanilla extract	**1/2 tsp**
Thandai syrup	**1/4 cup**
Egg yolk	**7 nos.**
Sugar (fine grain)	**fistful**
Water	**as required**

METHOD

- In a pan, add milk, cream, vanilla extract and thandai syrup. Bring the mix to a boil. Allow the mix to simmer for 2-3 minutes. Remove from heat.

- In a separate bowl, mix the egg yolks and sugar. Whisk till the sugar is dissolved.

- Now, gently pour the warm milk mix over the whisked eggs. Keep whisking.

- Pour the contents into the pan and let the mix simmer for 2-3 minutes. Keep stirring and remove from heat.

- Strain the contents and pour into oven-proof bowls. Place these bowls in a deep roasting tray filled with hot water up till 3/4th.

- In a preheated oven, bake at 160 degrees for 35 minutes.

- Remove from the oven and allow the tray to cool down. Keep it in the refrigerator so that it is properly chilled.

- Sprinkle fine grain sugar over the crème brûlée and using a blowtorch, caramelise the sugar for a crunchy top.

- Alternatively, in a pan, heat the sugar on low heat and caramelise it.

- Immediately, pour the caramelised sugar over the crème brûlée.

- Serve chilled.

Meal 04

serves

Guava & Mint Panna

•

Palak Soya Feta Parcels

•

Baked Tinda with Fennel Tomato Curry

•

Raw Mango Pulao

•

Green Apple Cinnamon Shrikhand with
Sesame Brittle

Guava & Mint Panna

INGREDIENTS

Guava juice (sweetened)	**500 ml**
Mint leaves	**1 cup**
Guava	**1 no.** (deseeded & diced)
Lemon	**1 no.**
Black salt	**1/2 tsp**
Salt	**to taste**
Cumin	**1 tbsp** (roasted & crushed)
Ice cubes	**few**

METHOD

- In a blender, add half of the guava juice along with mint leaves. Blend till the mint leaves have been properly and evenly crushed. Pour the juice into a punch bowl.

- Add the rest of the juice along with the diced guava.

- Squeeze lemon, sprinkle black salt, salt, cumin and add ice cubes to the juice.

- Stir and serve chilled.

Palak Soya Feta Parcels

INGREDIENTS

Butter	**a knob**
Onion	**1 no.** (small) (chopped)
Garlic	**2 tsp** (chopped)
Green chilli	**1 no.** (chopped)
Spinach	**1 bunch** (blanched & roughly chopped)
Cumin powder	**1 tsp**
Coriander powder	**2 tsp**
Turmeric	**1/2 tsp**
Red chilli powder	**1 tsp**
Salt	**to taste**
Cherry tomato	**1/2 cup** (halved)
Feta cheese	**100 gm**
Soya leaves	**few sprigs** (chopped)
Filo sheet	**12 nos.**

METHOD

- In a pan, melt butter. Add onion, garlic and green chilli. Sauté for a minute and then add spinach.

- Add all the remaining spices and cook for 3-4 minutes. Sprinkle salt and add cherry tomatoes. Toss and remove. Allow the mixture to cool down completely.

- Add cheese and soya leaves to the spinach mix.

- Spread a filo sheet and brush it with some butter. Place another sheet on top and cut into 4"x4" squares. Place the spinach filling in the centre. Fold the squares like little money bags/parcels.

- Preheat the oven at 180 degrees and bake till the parcels are brown.

- Remove and serve hot.

Baked Tinda with Fennel Tomato Curry

INGREDIENTS

Round gourd (*tinda*)	**6 nos.**
Turmeric	**1 tsp**
Chilli powder	**2 tsp**
Coriander powder	**2 tbsp**
Cumin powder	**1 tsp**
Dried fenugreek powder (*kasoori methi*)	**1 tsp**
Dry mango powder (*amchur*)	**4 tbsp**
Fennel seeds powder (*saunf*)	**2 tsp**
Black salt	**2 tsp**
Mustard oil	**1/2 cup**
Tomato juice	**600 ml**
Fennel seeds	**2 tsp**
Garlic	**5 cloves** (smashed)
Salt	**to taste**
Coriander	**few sprigs**

METHOD

- Scrape the tinda to peel a very thin layer of the skin. Remove the eye. Using a sharp knife, give a criss-cross slit on the bottom of the tinda.

- In a bowl, add all the powdered spices along with black salt and mix well.

- Pour mustard oil over the masala to make a runny paste. Add this masala between the slits of the tinda. Place these on a deep roasting tray and cook at 180 degrees in a preheated oven for 10 minutes.

- Pull out the tray and pour the tomato juice and sprinkle fennel seeds. Add garlic to the juice. Sprinkle salt and keep in the oven at 180 degrees for another 15 minutes.

- Carefully remove the tinda first and place on a serving dish.

- Pour the tomato curry and garnish with coriander sprigs. Serve hot.

Raw Mango Pulao

INGREDIENTS

Oil	2 tbsp
Dry red chilli	2 nos.
Mustard seeds	2 tsp
Asafoetida (*hing*)	a pinch
Curry leaves	few sprigs
Raw mango	1/2 cup (chopped)
Boiled basmati rice	2 cups
Salt	to taste
Water	as required

METHOD

- In a pan, heat oil. Add red chilli and mustard seeds. Once they pop, add asafoetida and give the mix a quick stir.

- Add curry leaves and then toss in the raw mangoes. Cook for 2 minutes.

- Add rice. Sprinkle salt and add little water enough to moisten up the rice. Toss the rice till sufficiently hot.

- Remove and serve hot.

Green Apple Cinnamon Shrikhand with Sesame Brittle

INGREDIENTS

Yoghurt	**2 cups**
Sugar	**2 tbsp**
Cinnamon powder	**1 tsp**
Green apple	**1 no.** (finely chopped)

FOR THE SESAME BRITTLE

Sugar	**1/2 cup**
Water	**1 tbsp**
Salt	**a tiny pinch**
White sesame seeds	**2 tbsp**
Black sesame seeds	**2 tbsp**
Butter (salted)	**1 tsp**

METHOD

- Hang the yoghurt in a muslin cloth for 2 hours. Remove and whisk the yoghurt along with sugar and cinnamon powder.

- Add apples to the yoghurt. Refrigerate the shrikhand till it is chilled.

- In another pan, add sugar, water and salt. Heat till the sugar caramelises.

- Add both white and black sesame seeds. Stir well. Add butter and give a quick stir.

- Pull out the contents on to a greased kitchen counter. Spread and allow the contents to cool down completely. Remove and place on a kitchen cloth and wrap the contents carefully. Whack with a rolling pin to crush the wrapped contents.

- Sprinkle the prepared mix over the chilled shrikhand and serve.

Meal 05

serves 2

Hibiscus, Rose & Basil Seed Sherbet

•

Asian Salad

•

Steamed Ginger Fish

•

Quick Fried Rice

•

Crisp Wanton with Matcha, Honey & Sesame

Hibiscus, Rose & Basil Seed Sherbet

INGREDIENTS

Hibiscus flower (dried)	6 nos.
Basil seeds	2 tsp
Sugar	3 tbsp
Hot water	2 cups
Ice cubes	as required
Rose water	few drops

METHOD

- Soak the hibiscus, basil seeds and sugar in hot water for 20 minutes. Allow the hibiscus to release its flavour, and the basil seeds to bloom.

- Place sufficient ice cubes in 2 glasses and pour the hibiscus drink over the ice evenly.

- Add a few drops of rose water. Stir well and serve.

Asian Salad

INGREDIENTS

Cucumber	**1 no.** (small) (peeled in thin strips)
Carrot	**1 no.** (small) (peeled in thin strips)
Red cabbage	**1/4 no.** (small) (finely shredded)
Lettuce leaves	**handful** (broken into bite-size pieces)
Pineapple	**1 cup** (diced)
Onion	**1 no.** (small) (sliced)
Ginger	**2 tsp** (chopped)
Honey	**3 tbsp**
Lemon	**6 tbsp**
Soya sauce (light)	**3 tbsp**
Chilli sauce	**2 tsp**
Sesame oil	**1 tbsp**
Salt	**to taste**
Sesame seeds	**2 tbsp** (toasted)
Cashew nuts	**handful** (roasted)

METHOD

- In a bowl, add thin strips of cucumber and carrot.

- Add shredded red cabbage, lettuce, pineapple and onions.

- Separately whisk ginger, honey, lemon, soya sauce, chilli sauce and sesame oil together.

- Pour the mix over the veggies. Sprinkle a little salt.

- Add sesame seeds and cashew nuts. Toss the salad.

- Mix well and serve immediately.

Steamed Ginger Fish

INGREDIENTS

Fish fillet	**2 nos.** (200 gm each)
Salt	**to taste**
White pepper powder	**a generous pinch**
Sugar	**1 tsp**
Soya sauce	**1/4 cup** (light)
Ginger	**1/2 cup** (julienned)
Spring onion	**1 stalk** (julienned)
Oil	**4 tbsp**
Garlic	**5 cloves** (smashed & chopped)
Red chilli	**1 no.** (julienned)
Sesame oil	**1 tbsp**

METHOD

- Pat dry the fish and remove all the bones.

- Marinate the fish with salt, white pepper powder, sugar, soya sauce, half of ginger (reserve the rest) and half of spring onion juliennes.

- On a plate, place the fish with the marinade. Ready the steamer and cook for about 12 minutes or till the fish is done.

- Remove the plate carefully and do not discard the juices of the steamed, cooked fish.

- In a separate pan, heat oil till it smokes.

- Remove the pan from the heat and add garlic, the remaining ginger juliennes, red chilli and spring onions. Stir the mix and add sesame oil. Pour the mix over the fish evenly.

- Serve hot with extra soya sauce on the side.

Quick Fried Rice

INGREDIENTS

Oil	**2 tbsp**
Garlic	**1 tsp** (chopped)
Onion	**2 tbsp** (chopped)
Ginger	**1 tsp** (chopped)
Green chilli	**1/2 no.** (chopped)
Carrot	**2 tbsp** (chopped)
Cabbage	**2 tbsp** (chopped)
Beans	**2 tbsp** (chopped)
Red pepper	**1 tbsp**
Boiled rice	**2 cups**
Salt	**a pinch**
Pepper	**a pinch**
Soya sauce	**2 tbsp**
Vinegar	**1 tsp**
Water	**as required**
Spring onion	**1/4 cup** (chopped)

METHOD

- Heat a pan on high flame. Add oil followed by garlic. Quickly stir and add onions, ginger and green chilli. Toss for a minute.

- Add carrots, cabbage, beans and red pepper. Give a quick stir.

- Add boiled rice followed by a pinch of salt, pepper, soya sauce, vinegar and water.

- Toss the rice gently on high flame for about 3 minutes. Turn off the heat and add spring onions.

- Toss well and serve hot.

Crisp Wanton with Matcha, Honey & Sesame

INGREDIENTS

Wanton sheet (3"x3")	**10 nos.**
Oil	**for deep frying**
Honey	**5 tbsp**
Water	**as required**
Peanuts	**handful** (toasted)
Matcha powder	**2 tbsp**
Black sesame seeds	**1 tbsp**
White sesame seeds	**1 tbsp**

METHOD

- Cut the wanton into 1 cm-wide strips.

- In a pan, heat oil. Deep fry the strips till crisp and remove.

- In a separate pan, add honey with equal quantity of water
and bring to a boil. Add peanuts and allow the mix to thicken.

- Remove and drizzle the mix over the crisp wantons. Dust with
matcha powder.

- Before serving, sprinkle black and white sesame seeds over
the crisps.

Meal 06

serves

Kohlrabi Slaw

•

Gold Drink

•

Lamb Curry in Pickling Spices

•

Khameeri Roti

•

Mango in Chocolate Cups

Kohlrabi Slaw

INGREDIENTS

Apple	**1 no.**
Kohlrabi	**3 nos.**
Cabbage	**1/4 no.** (large) (finely shredded)
Onion	**1 no.** (small) (sliced)
Sugar	**2 tsp**
Salt	**a generous pinch**
Pepper	**a pinch**
Lemon	**1 no.**
Mayonnaise	**2 tbsp**
Walnuts	**handful** (toasted)
Coriander	**few sprigs**

METHOD

- Cut the apple into matchstick sizes and keep aside.

- Peel the kohlrabi and cut into matchstick sizes. Keep aside.

- In a large bowl, combine the kohlrabi with cabbage, onions, sugar, salt, pepper and lemon juice. Leave the slaw for 5 minutes.

- Next, squeeze out the excess water and add mayonnaise, walnuts and apples over the slaw. Make sure the dressing is evenly coated.

- Mix well, garnish with coriander and serve.

Gold Drink

INGREDIENTS

Champagne	**1/2 bottle** (chilled)
Gold leaf (3"x3")	**6 nos.**
Angostura bitters	**few drops**
Gooseberry	**handful**

METHOD

- In a bowl, pour 150 ml chilled champagne.

- Add 4 gold leaves to the champagne. Next, using a fork, dip the leaves and whisk vigorously. The leaves will break into smaller flakes.

- Now, pour this mix into the champagne glasses. Drizzle with Angostura bitters and top up with the rest of the chilled champagne.

- Roll the gooseberries with the remaining gold leaves.

- Drop the gooseberries into the champagne and serve chilled.

Lamb Curry in Pickling Spices

INGREDIENTS

Cumin seeds	**1 tbsp**
Fennel seeds (*saunf*)	**1/2 tbsp**
Fenugreek seeds (*methi*)	**1/2 tbsp**
Nigella seeds (*kalonji*)	**1/2 tbsp**
Mustard seeds	**1/2 tbsp**
Mutton (on bone)	**400 gm**
Onion	**1 no.** (large) (peeled & sliced)
Peppercorns	**7-8 nos.**
Ghee/Oil	**1/4 cup**
Yoghurt	**2½ cups**
Ginger paste	**2 tbsp**
Garlic paste	**2 tbsp**
Salt	**to taste**
Coriander powder	**2 tbsp**
Water	**2 cups**
Green chilli (thick ones used for pickles)	**6 nos.** (slit)

METHOD

- In a preheated pan, dry roast the cumin, fennel seeds, fenugreek seeds, nigella seeds and mustard seeds for 2-3 minutes. Remove and using a rolling pin, crush the mix coarsely.

- Place the mutton in a bowl and add onions, peppercorns, ghee, whisked yoghurt, ginger-garlic paste, salt and coriander powder. Mix well and pour it into a thick-bottom pan. Sprinkle the coarsely crushed masala on top.

- Cover the pan and cook on high heat till it gets to a boil. Allow the mutton to simmer, while covered. Keep stirring at regular intervals.

- Add water and cook till the meat is almost tender. At this stage, drop the green chillies in the curry and cook for another 10 minutes.

- Check for the seasoning and remove.

- Serve hot.

Khameeri Roti

INGREDIENTS

Milk (lukewarm)	**2/3 cups**
Fresh yeast	**1 tsp**
Sugar	**1 tsp**
Refined flour	**2½ cups**
Salt	**a generous pinch**
Baking powder	**1/2 tsp**
Nigella seeds (*kalonji*)	**1 tbsp**
Pumpkin seeds	**1 tbsp**
Sesame seeds	**1 tbsp**
Coriander	**2 tbsp** (chopped)
Water	**as required**

NOTES

If the bread falls off, please add water again on the back of the bread and heat the pan on high flame and stick the bread again. The bread can also be baked at 220 degrees in an oven.

METHOD

- In luke warm milk, add yeast, sugar and 1 tablespoon of refined flour. Store in a warm place for about 30 minutes so that the milk starts bubbling.

- Now, using this milk mix, make a dough with 2 cups flour mixed with salt and baking powder. Use some water if required. Make a smooth dough. Allow to rest for 5 minutes. Divide into 4 equal-sized balls and allow these to rest for 20 minutes.

- Roll these out about 1 cm in thickness, using the remaining flour. Baste the top of the bread with water.

- Sprinkle nigella seeds, pumpkin seeds, sesame seeds and coriander. Press gently so they stick to the bread.

- Heat a pan/tawa on high flame. Pick the rolled bread and place it on your palm with the garnished side facing down. Wet the other hand with water and gently pat the back of the bread. Place the bread on the preheated pan. Make sure that the garnished side of the bread is facing upwards.

- Hover the upturned pan/tawa over the flame so that the flame cooks the bread evenly.

- Once the top of the bread puffs up and browns a bit, place the pan back on the stove and cook for another minute.

- Using a pair of tongs, remove the bread and repeat with the remaining dough.

- Serve hot.

Mango in Chocolate Cups

INGREDIENTS

Dark chocolate chips	**2 cups**
Muffin moulds (paper)	**few**
Cream	**1/2 cup**
Cream cheese	**1/2 cup**
Mango	**1/2 cup** (diced)
Sugar	**1/4 cup**

METHOD

- Melt the dark chocolate in a microwave. Once melted, pour into muffin moulds and fill them up completely. Upturn the moulds immediately to drain out all the chocolate. At the same time, the chocolate should coat the moulds evenly. Allow to set in the refrigerator.

- In a bowl, add cream and cream cheese. Whisk well.

- In a blender, add mangos and sugar. Make a thick purée. Remove and mix the purée with cream and cheese. Refrigerate for an hour.

- Peel off the paper cups off the moulds to reveal the chocolate cups.

- Pour the mango mixture on these cups.

- Serve chilled.

Meal 07

serves

Apple & Walnut Salad

•

Turnip Purée with Chilli Garlic Bread

•

Mustard Leaf Mash

•

Radish & Cornmeal Roti

•

Garbar Falooda

Apple & Walnut Salad

INGREDIENTS

Sugar	**½ cup**
Walnuts	**handful** (crushed)
Red wine	**½ bottle**
Apple	**2 nos.** (sliced into wedges)
Leafy greens (mixed)	**1 small bunch**
Rocket leaves	**1 bunch**
Salt	**a pinch**
Pepper	**a pinch**
Lemon	**1 no.**
Olive oil	**1 tbsp**
Feta cheese	**50 gm** (crumbled)

METHOD

- In a non-stick pan, add sugar and heat it on low flame. Allow the sugar to caramelise.

- Once the sugar attains an amber colour, add walnuts. Stir well so that the walnuts are evenly coated. Turn off the heat and keep aside. Allow the nuts to cool down and solidify.

- Next, using a rolling pin, crush the sugar and the walnuts. Keep aside.

- In a separate saucepan, pour red wine and bring to a boil. Add apple wedges to the wine and cook on high flame to reduce it. Once the wine reduces sufficiently and the apple wedges have been evenly coated, remove from heat and keep aside. Allow to cool down completely.

- Wash the greens, shake off the excess water and place in a bowl.

- Add salt, pepper, lemon and olive oil. Toss the mix gently.

- Add apples along with the reduced wine, cheese and walnuts.

- Serve immediately.

Turnip Purée with Chilli Garlic Bread

INGREDIENTS

For the Chilli Garlic Bread

French loaf	**1/2 no.**
Garlic	**5 cloves** (crushed)
Basil	**few sprigs** (chopped)
Butter	**3 tbsp**
Chilli flakes	**1 tbsp**

For the Turnip Purée

Ghee	**4 tbsp**
Fennel seeds (*saunf*)	**1 tsp**
Fenugreek seeds (*methi*)	**1 tsp**
Turnip (*shalgum*)	**6 nos.** (peeled & quartered)
Turmeric	**1/2 tsp**
Salt	**to taste**
Chilli powder	**1 tsp**
Sugar	**2 tbsp**
Water	**½ cup**
Basil	**few sprigs**
Parmesan cheese	**1/3 cup** (grated)

METHOD

- Slice the bread lengthwise to make sticks. Mix garlic, basil, butter and chilli flakes in a bowl. Baste the breadsticks with this mix and place them in the oven at 120 degrees for half hour to make them crisp.

- For the purée, in a pan, heat ghee. Add fennel and fenugreek seeds. Stir well.

- Add turnips and stir for a minute.

- Add turmeric, salt, chilli powder and sugar. Cook for 3-4 minutes.

- Add water and cover. Cook on low heat till the turnips are very tender. Using a large ladle, mash the turnip and mix thoroughly. Cook for another 3-4 minutes to dry up excess moisture. Once the mix achieves a mash-like consistency, remove from heat.

- Add basil and parmesan cheese.

- Toss and serve with the crisp bread.

Mustard Leaf Mash

INGREDIENTS

Split chickpeas (*chana dal*)	**1/3 cup** (washed & soaked)
Turnip (*shalgum*)	**1 no.** (large) (peeled & cut into small cubes)
Water	**2 cups**
Mustard leaves	**1 large bunch** (washed)
Spinach	**1/4 bunch** (washed)
Bathua leaves	**handful** (washed)
Radish leaves	**handful** (washed)
Fenugreek leaves (*methi*)	**handful** (washed)
Green chilli	**2 nos.**

For Tempering

Ghee	**3 tbsp**
Garlic	**1 tbsp** (chopped)
Onion	**3 tbsp** (chopped)
Ginger	**1 tbsp** (chopped)
Chilli powder	**1 tsp**
Salt	**to taste**
Butter	**a knob**

METHOD

- In a vessel, add split chickpeas and turnips along with water. Cook covered till the chickpeas are almost done.

- At this stage, add all the green leaves and green chilli. Bring this mix to a boil and cook till all the leaves wilt. This should not take more than a few minutes. Remove from heat and allow to cool down partially.

- Put all the contents into a food processor and prepare a purée.

- In a fresh pan, heat ghee.

- Add garlic and cook till it begins to brown. Add onions and ginger and cook till brown.

- Next, add chilli powder and stir well. Add the previously prepared purée immediately. Cook for 12-15 minutes. Add salt and stir well.

- Remove and serve hot with butter.

Radish & Cornmeal Roti

INGREDIENTS

Salt	to taste
Radish	1 no. (small) (peeled & grated)
Maize flour	2 cups
Radish leaves	few (finely chopped)
Green chilli	1 no. (finely chopped)
Water	as required
Plastic film	2 nos.
Ghee	1/4 cup

METHOD

- Add 1/2 tsp salt to the radish and leave aside for 5 minutes. Squeeze out the excess water from the grated radish.

- In a bowl, add flour, a pinch of salt, grated radish, radish leaves and green chilli. Add water to make a dough. Divide the dough into 4 equal-sized balls.

- Place a plastic film/sheet on the kitchen table and lightly oil it. Place the dough and cover it with another oiled plastic film and flatten it out using your hands.

- Remove the film and carefully place it on a hot griddle or a pan and cook the roti on both sides using ghee.

- Serve hot.

NOTES

The bread will have some cracked edges but that is how it should be. Do not roll out very thin as the bread might break. Grated radish holds the dough together and lends the roti a good sharp taste.

Garbar Falooda

INGREDIENTS

Basil seeds	2 tbsp
Water	1 cup
Milk (full cream)	1 litre
Sugar	2½ tbsp
Screw pine flower water (*kewra*) (light)	2 tbsp
Khus syrup	3 tbsp
Rose syrup	3 tbsp
Falooda	2 cups
Candied fruits	handful
Jujubes	handful
Gummy bears	handful
Berries (assorted)	1/2 cup
Crushed ice	1 cup

METHOD

- Soak the basil seeds in a cup of water till they bloom.

- For making the rabri, in a pan, pour milk and cook on low heat while stirring continuously till it reduces to 1/3rd.

- Once the milk reduces, add sugar and remove from heat. Keep the rabri in the refrigerator.

- Once cold, add kewra water to the rabri.

- Separately, line the sides of 2 tall glasses with khus and rose syrup.

- Add 1/2 of the falooda to the glasses equally, followed by a big spoon of rabri.

- Add basil seeds, candied fruits, jujubes and gummy bears. Add berries and repeat the process. Top up with crushed ice.

- Serve immediately.

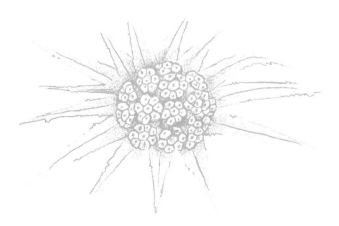

Meal 08

serves

Raw Papaya & Raw Mango Salad

•

Crumb Fried Paneer

•

Potato & Mango Curry

•

Sattu Parantha with Wasabi Butter

•

Goji Berry Yoghurt Parfait

Raw Papaya & Raw Mango Salad

INGREDIENTS

Raw papaya	1 no. (small)
Raw mango	1 no. (large)
Carrot	2 nos. (medium)
Garlic	2 cloves
Green chilli	1/2 no.
Jaggery	5 tbsp (powdered)
Lemon	2 nos.
Salt	to taste
Coriander	few sprigs

METHOD

- Peel the papaya, mango and carrots. Cut these into thin long strips. Pile the strips on top of each other and then cut them lengthwise into thin strips. Put these strips in a bowl and keep aside.

- Crush the garlic cloves, green chilli and jaggery using a mortar and a pestle.

- Add lemon juice and salt. Mix all the ingredients till the jaggery is dissolved.

- Pour this dressing over the salad.

- Toss and serve cold, garnished with coriander.

Crumb Fried Paneer

INGREDIENTS

Paneer	**1½ cups** (diced)
Salt	**to taste**
Turmeric	**a pinch**
Asafoetida (*hing*)	**a pinch**
Red chilli powder	**1 tsp**
Ginger-garlic paste	**2 tbsp**
Refined flour	**1 cup**
Water	**as required**
Breadcrumbs	**as required**
Oil	**for frying**
Chaat masala	**a generous pinch**
Coriander	**few sprigs**

METHOD

- Marinate the paneer with salt, turmeric, asafoetida, red chilli powder and ginger-garlic paste. Keep aside for 5 minutes.

- Make a thick batter with 4 tablespoons of flour and 4 tablespoons of water and season the batter with salt. Keep aside.

- Lightly coat the paneer with dry, refined flour. Dust off the excess flour from the paneer cubes.

- Drop the cubes into the batter for a light coating.

- Remove a few cubes from the batter and shake off the excess. Add to the breadcrumbs and make sure the cubes are coated evenly. Gently press the breadcrumbs if required. Repeat the process with the remaining paneer cubes.

- In a pan, heat oil. Deep fry the paneer cubes till crispy and golden. Remove and sprinkle chaat masala over the paneer.

- Serve hot, garnished with coriander.

Potato & Mango Curry

INGREDIENTS

Water	**as required** (for boiling)
Salt	**to taste**
Potato	**2 nos.** (large) (peeled & diced)
Oil	**3 tbsp**
Dry red chilli	**1 no.**
Asafoetida (*hing*)	**1 tsp**
Mustard seeds	**1 tsp**
Cumin seeds	**1 tsp**
Curry leaves	**5 sprigs**
Green chilli	**1 no.** (slit)
Ginger	**1 small knob** (finely chopped)
Onion	**1 no.** (small) (finely chopped)
Raw mango (sour)	**3 nos.** (small) (diced)
Turmeric	**1 tsp**
Chilli powder	**2 tsp**
Mango juice (sweetened)	**500 ml**

METHOD

- In a wok, add water, a generous pinch of salt and potatoes. Boil till the potatoes are done. Remove and keep aside.

- In a separate pan, heat oil and add dry red chilli. Sauté and add asafoetida.

- Add mustard and cumin seeds. Once the seeds begin to splutter, add curry leaves and sauté.

- Add green chilli and ginger. Toss the mix gently for 30 seconds.

- Add onions to the mix and sauté for a minute before adding the raw mangoes.

- Sprinkle turmeric, chilli powder and salt. Sauté and add potatoes. Gently toss the mix and add mango juice.

- Simmer on low flame till the curry thickens.

- Serve hot.

Sattu Parantha with Wasabi Butter

INGREDIENTS

Wheat	**¼ cup** (soaked overnight)
Whole wheat flour	**2½ cups**
Oats	**¼ cup**
Salt	**a generous pinch**
Water	**as required**
Red chilli pickle	**½ no.**
Split chickpeas flour (*sattu chana*)	**1 cup**
Onion	**1 no.** (small) (finely chopped)
Coriander	**1 tbsp** (chopped)
Caraway seeds (*ajwain*)	**1 tsp**
Nigella seeds (*kalonji*)	**1 tsp**
Garlic	**2 tsp** (chopped)
Mustard oil	**2 tbsp**
Clarified butter (*ghee*)	**3 tbsp**

FOR THE WASABI BUTTER

Wasabi paste	**1 tsp**
Butter	**50 gm** (softened, not melted)

METHOD

- Using a rolling pin, roughly crush the soaked wheat.

- In a bowl, add 2 cups of whole wheat flour, soaked wheat, oats and salt. Mix well. Add enough water to make a stiff dough. Leave it to rest for 10 minutes. Divide the dough into 4 large-sized balls and keep aside for another 10 minutes.

- On a chopping board, place the red chilli pickle and using a knife, chop it along with its masala. Make sure it is as fine as possible.

- For the stuffing, in a separate bowl, add sattu, onions, red chilli pickle, coriander, caraway and nigella seeds, garlic and mustard oil. Mix well. Add a dash of water if required to make a moist, crumbly filling.

- Stuff the dough with the sattu mixture. Using a rolling pin, make flat thin discs.

- On a preheated pan, cook the sattu parantha with ghee on both sides.

- For the wasabi butter, add wasabi paste to the softened butter and mix well.

- Put a dollop of the wasabi butter-mix on a butter paper and refrigerate.

- Serve the piping hot paranthas with wasabi butter.

Goji Berry Yoghurt Parfait

INGREDIENTS

Yoghurt (thick)	**1½ cups**
Sugar	**2 tbsp**
Vanilla extract	**1 tsp**
Honey	**1 tbsp**
Goji berry (dried)	**4 tbsp**
Basil	**few sprigs**
Water	**as required**

METHOD

- In a bowl, add yoghurt, sugar and vanilla extract. Whisk well and pour the mix into 2 glasses.

- In a separate pan, add honey, goji berries, basil and 6 tablespoons of water. Mix and allow to simmer on low heat till the berries bloom and acquire a nice glaze.

- Do not dry up the berries completely, let these be a little syrupy. Add more water if required. Remove from heat and keep aside.

- Add a generous portion of the berries on top of the yoghurt and serve chilled.

Meal 09

serves

Watermelon, Mint & Ginger Slushie

•

Asparagus & Beans Crisps

•

Spinach & Apricot Kofta with
Pumpkin Tomato Sauce

•

Orange & Mint Pulao

•

Apple Cinnamon Parantha with
Custard Sauce

Watermelon, Mint & Ginger Slushie

INGREDIENTS

Watermelon	**4 cups** (diced)
Ice cube	**10 nos.**
Sugar	**4 tbsp** (powdered)
Mint leaves	**1 cup**
Ginger	**2 tsp** (chopped)
Lemon	**1 no.**

METHOD

- Place the diced watermelon in a deep freezer. Let the watermelon be completely frozen.

- In a blender, add frozen watermelon along with ice cubes, sugar, mint leaves and ginger. Squeeze a lemon and blend to make an iced slushie.

- Serve immediately.

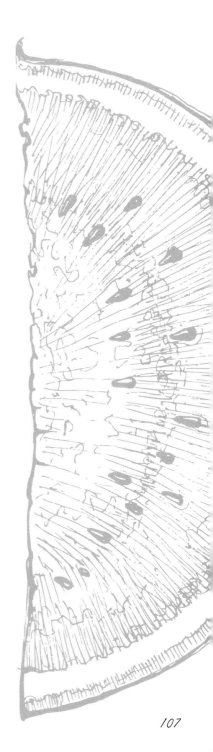

Asparagus & Beans Crisps

INGREDIENTS

Butter	**1 tbsp**
Nigella seeds (*kalonji*)	**1 tsp**
Garlic	**2 cloves** (smashed & chopped)
Onion	**1 no.** (small) (finely chopped)
Green chilli	**1 no.** (finely chopped)
Asparagus	**4 stalks** (finely chopped)
Beans	**4 stalks** (finely chopped)
Salt	**to taste**
Spring roll sheet	**6 nos.**
Water	**as required**
Oil	**to fry**

METHOD

- In a pan, melt butter and add nigella seeds.

- Add garlic, onions and green chilli. Cook for a minute on medium flame.

- Add asparagus, beans and salt. Cook for 4 minutes on low flame or till the beans are tender and yet retain the bite. Remove and allow to cool down completely.

- Separately, cut the spring roll sheet diagonally into a triangular shape.

- Place a spoonful of the stuffing in the centre of the sheet. Apply little water on all the edges of the sheet. Fold from the sides and carefully roll the sheet like a cigar. Press the edges to seal.

- In a separate pan, heat oil and deep fry these cigar-shaped crisps till done.

- Remove and serve hot.

Spinach & Apricot Kofta with Pumpkin Tomato Sauce

INGREDIENTS

FOR THE KOFTA

Ghee	1/4 cup
Cumin	1 tsp
Garlic	1 tbsp (chopped)
Green chilli	1 no.
Coriander powder	2 tsp
Spinach purée (thick)	1 cup
Potato	1/2 cup (boiled & mashed)
Salt	to taste
Dried apricot	1/2 cup (chopped)
Breadcrumbs	for coating

FOR THE SAUCE

Oil	1/4 cup
Tomato	500 gm
Pumpkin	150 gm
Onion	1 no. (small)
Ginger	a knob
Garlic	5 cloves
Cashew nuts	1/4 cup
Green chilli	1 no
Water	2 cups
Butter	2 tbsp
Kashmiri chilli powder	2 tsp
Salt	to taste
Fenugreek leaves powder (*methi*)	1 tsp
Garam masala powder	a pinch
Cream	1/4 cup

METHOD

- In a vessel, heat ghee and add cumin. Once it begins to crackle, add garlic and green chilli. Cook till the garlic turns light brown.

- Add coriander powder and immediately add spinach purée. Cook for 8-10 minutes or till the spinach becomes thick. Remove and allow the mix to cool down. Once cooled, add mashed potatoes, salt and dried apricots. Mix well.

- Divide the mix into small balls and coat with breadcrumbs. In a separate pan, deep fry the spinach and apricot koftas till brown.

- For the sauce/curry, in a bowl, mix tomatoes, pumpkin, onion, ginger, garlic, cashew nuts, green chilli and water together.

- Boil the above mix for 30 minutes. Purée and strain it.

- In a separate vessel, melt butter, add kashmiri chilli powder and immediately add the prepared purée. Cook for 15 minutes on medium heat.

- Add water to get a thick but a pouring consistency. Add salt, fenugreek leaves powder and garam masala powder. Turn off the heat and add cream. Stir and pour the curry into a bowl and drop in the previously prepared koftas.

- Serve hot.

Orange & Mint Pulao

INGREDIENTS

Oil	**3 tbsp**
Bay leaf	**1 no.**
Peppercorns	**5 nos.**
Cinnamon	**1 stick**
Caraway seeds (*shahi jeera*)	**1 tsp**
Onion	**1 no.** (small) (peeled & sliced)
Garlic	**3 cloves** (sliced)
Green chilli	**2 nos.**
Orange	**2 nos.** (cut, deseeded & juice extracted)
Basmati rice	**1 cup** (washed & soaked for 1/2 hour)
Water	**2 cups**
Salt	**to taste**
Mint leaves	**1 cup**

METHOD

- Heat a pan and add oil.

- Add bay leaf, peppercorns, cinnamon and caraway seeds. Stir well.

- Add onions and cook until browned.

- Add garlic and green chilli. Cook for a few seconds. Add squeezed orange rind and juice and give a quick stir.

- Add soaked rice and water along with salt. Bring to a boil.

- Add mint leaves and lower the heat.

- Cover and cook till the rice is done and the water is absorbed.

- Remove the orange rind and serve hot.

Apple Cinnamon Parantha with Custard Sauce

INGREDIENTS

FOR THE DOUGH

Whole wheat flour	2½ cups
Salt	a pinch
Ghee	4 tbsp
Water	as required

FOR THE STUFFING

Apple	2 nos. (deseeded & diced)
Brown sugar	4 tbsp
Cinnamon powder	2 tsp
Bread	2 slices (sides removed)
Butter (salted)	1 tbsp
Lemon	1 no. (small)

FOR THE CUSTARD SAUCE

Milk	1 cup
Cream	1 cup
Sugar	1/2 cup
Egg yolk	3 nos.
Vanilla extract	1 tsp
Icing sugar	for garnish
Mint leaves	for garnish

METHOD

- Mix 2 cups of whole wheat flour, salt and 1 tablespoon of ghee together. Add sufficient water to make a stiff dough. Allow to rest and then divide the dough into 4 equal-sized balls. Keep aside.

- In a bowl, add apples. Add brown sugar, cinnamon powder and mix well.

- In a blender, add bread slices. Blend the slices into crumbs.

- Heat a pan and add butter. Once it melts, add apples and cook on high flame for 3 minutes.

- Squeeze a lemon and add breadcrumbs. Toss till the mixture comes together. Remove and refrigerate the mix.

- Stuff the previously prepared dough balls with a generous helping of the apple mixture. Using the remaining flour, roll the dough balls into circular discs.

- In a pan, cook the apple cinnamon parantha using desi ghee. Make sure the parantha is crisp on both sides. Remove and slice it like a pizza.

- For the custard sauce, mix milk, cream and sugar together. Bring to a boil and remove.

- In a bowl, add egg yolks and vanilla extract. Whisk well. Pour 3 ladles of warm milk on the yolks while still whisking.

- Add the yolks back into the milk and heat the mix. Stir continuously till it reaches a quick gentle boil. Remove from heat immediately. Allow to cool and chill in the refrigerator.

- Dust the warm apple cinnamon parantha with icing sugar.

- Garnish with mint leaves and serve with the custard sauce.

Meal 10

serves

Avocado, Blueberry & Mint Lassi

•

Dal Pakwan Tower with

Tamarind Date Chutney

•

Bhuna Pyaaz

•

Methi Roti

•

Chocolate Ganache &
Orange Chutney Tarts

Avocado, Blueberry & Mint Lassi

INGREDIENTS

Avocado	**1 no.** (small)
	(deseeded & halved)
Yoghurt	**2 cups**
Blueberry	**1/2 cup**
Mint leaves	**1/2 cup**
Honey	**4 tbsp**
Vanilla extract	**1 tsp**
Ice cube	**10 nos.**

METHOD

- Remove the pulp from the avocado.

- In a blender, add avocado, yoghurt, blueberries, mint leaves, honey, vanilla extract and ice cubes. Mix and blend till smooth.

- Remove and serve chilled.

Dal Pakwan Tower with Tamarind Date Chutney

INGREDIENTS

FOR THE DAL

Split chickpeas (*chana dal*)	1 cup
Water	as required
Salt	to taste
Turmeric	1/2 tsp
Green chilli	2 nos.
Ghee	4 tbsp
Cumin seeds	2 tsp
Curry leaves	few sprigs

FOR THE PAKWAN

Refined flour	2 cups
Salt	1/2 tsp
Cumin	1 tsp
Ghee	4 tbsp
Milk	1/2 cup
Water	as required
Oil	for deep frying

FOR THE TAMARIND DATE CHUTNEY

Tamarind	2 cups
Date	12 nos. (deseeded)
Water	8 cups
Sugar	1 cup
Salt	to taste
Black salt	1½ tsp
Cumin	1 tbsp (roasted)
Chilli powder	2 tsp

FOR GARNISH

Onion	½ **cup** (chopped)
Tomato	½ **cup** (chopped)
Coriander	¼ **cup** (chopped)
Mint leaves	handful
Salt	to taste
Lemon	2 nos.
Sour cream	½ cup
Jalapeños	handful

METHOD

- Wash the chickpeas and soak for 45 minutes. Drain the water and add thrice the quantity of fresh water with salt, turmeric and green chillies. Cover and boil till the dal is tender and yet whole and not mashed. Remove from heat.

- In a separate pan, heat ghee. Add cumin seeds and once they begin to splutter, add curry leaves.

- Add tempering to the dal and cook for 5-8 minutes. Once the dal thickens, remove from heat.

- For the pakwan, in a bowl, add flour, salt, cumin and ghee. Mix well. Using milk and a little water, make a stiff dough. Allow to rest for 15 minutes.

- Roll out the dough thin. Using a fork, dock it in different places. Cut into triangular shapes like nachos.

- In a separate pan, heat oil and deep fry the pakwan till crisp. Remove and keep aside.

- For the tamarind date chutney, soak the tamarind in water for 20 minutes.

- In a pan, add tamarind with water.

- Add all the remaining ingredients and boil for 30 minutes on low flame, covered.

- Add water if the mix turns too thick. When the chutney thickens enough to coat the back of a spoon, remove from heat and strain. Keep aside.

- For the garnish, in a separate bowl, add onions, tomatoes, coriander, mint leaves, salt and lemon juice. Keep this tomato salsa aside for later.

- Place 1/3rd of the previously fried pakwan like a heap on a platter.

- Drizzle 1/3rd of the prepared dal on top, pour a little sour cream and tamarind chutney.

- Sprinkle a little tomato salsa and jalapeños.

- Serve immediately.

121

Bhuna Pyaaz

INGREDIENTS

For Roasting Onions

Turmeric	1 tsp
Chilli powder	2 tsp
Coriander powder	2 tbsp
Cumin powder	1 tsp

For the Masala

Oil	4 tbsp
Mustard seeds	2 tsp
Cumin seeds	2 tsp
Nigella seeds (*kalonji*)	1 tsp
Fennel seeds (*saunf*)	2 tsp
Fenugreek seeds (*methi*)	1 tsp
Asafoetida (*hing*)	1/2 tsp
Onion	1½ cups (chopped)
Ginger	2 tbsp (chopped)
Garlic	2 tbsp (chopped)
Green chilli	1 no. (slit)
Turmeric	1/2 tsp
Red chilli powder	1 tsp
Coriander powder	1 tbsp
Water	as required
Tomato	3 cups (chopped)
Salt	to taste
Mango pickle	4-5 pieces
Coriander leaves	for garnish

Fenugreek leaves powder (*methi*)	1 tsp
Black salt	2 tsp
Dry mango powder (*amchur*)	4 tbsp
Salt	to taste
Mustard oil	1/2 cup
Onion	6 nos. (peeled, criss-cross slit)

METHOD

- In a bowl, add all the spices (under roasting onions) along with salt and mustard oil. Mix well and keep this masala aside.

- Stuff onions with the prepared masala. Place these on a roasting tray and cook at 180 degrees in an oven for 20 minutes.

- Heat a pan, add oil. Add mustard, cumin, nigella, fennel and fenugreek seeds. Cook for 10 seconds.

- Next, sprinkle asafoetida, stir and add chopped onions.

- Cook the onions till browned. At this stage, add ginger, garlic and green chillies. Cook for 2 minutes.

- In a separate bowl, add turmeric, red chilli powder and coriander powder with a little water. Mix well. Add this masala to the pan. Cook for 2 minutes and add tomatoes.

- Sprinkle salt and cook for another 10 minutes. Add a cup of water and cook till the mix reaches a boil. Lower the heat.

- Roughly chop the mango pickle and add to the masala. Allow the mix to thicken a bit. Remove from heat and pour the masala in a bowl.

- Add the previously prepared roasted onions on top and garnish with coriander leaves.

- Serve hot.

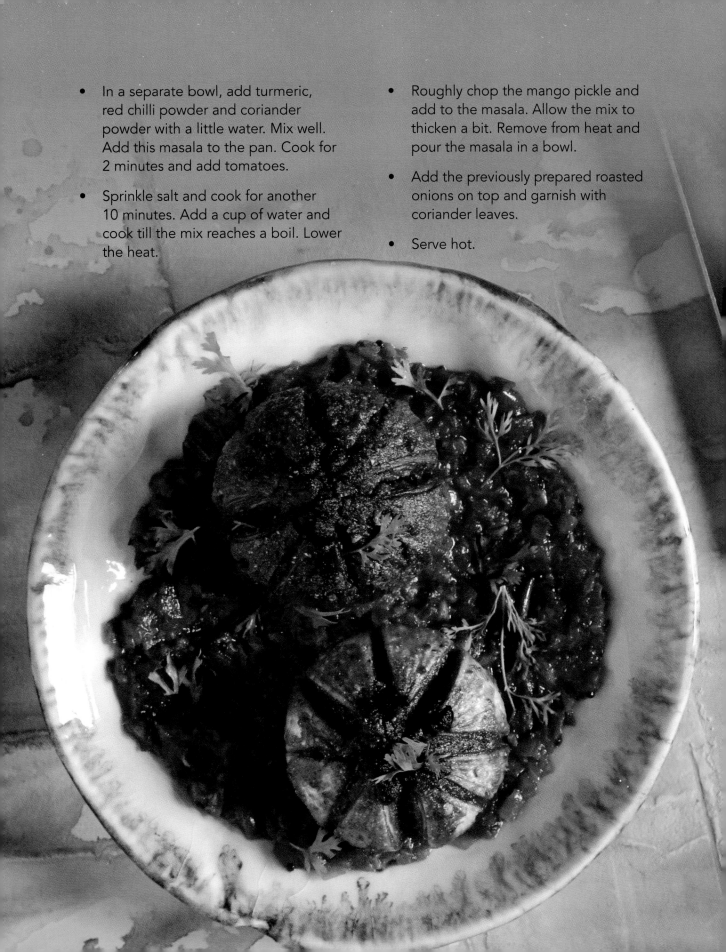

Methi Roti

INGREDIENTS

Whole wheat flour	**2½ cups**
Salt	**a generous pinch**
Fenugreek leaves (*methi*)	**1 cup** (washed & roughly chopped)
Onion	**1/4 cup** (chopped)
Green chilli	**1 no.** (chopped)
Carom seeds (*ajwain*)	**1 tsp**
Water	**3/4 cup**
Ghee	**1/2 cup**

METHOD

- In a bowl, add 2 cups of flour, salt, fenugreek leaves, onions, green chilli, carom seeds and water. Make a soft dough and keep aside for 10 minutes.

- Knead again and divide the dough into 4 equal-sized balls. Dust using the remaining flour and roll them out flat.

- Heat a pan and cook the roti on both sides. Give 2 minutes to each side.

- Remove, apply ghee and serve hot.

Chocolate Ganache & Orange Chutney Tarts

INGREDIENTS

For the Short Crust Pastry

Flour	**1½ cups**
Butter (salted)	**1/2 cup**
Sugar	**1 tbsp**
Thyme	**few sprigs**
Orange rind	**of 1 orange**
Water (chilled)	**as required**
Moulds	**as required**

For the Chutney

Orange (valencia or mandarin)	**2 nos.** (quartered with skin)
Sugar	**1 cup**
Cinnamon	**1 stick**
Salt	**a pinch**
Red chilli powder	**a pinch** (optional)
Water	**5 cups**

For the Chocolate ganache

Dark chocolate	**200 gm** (broken into small pieces)
Fresh cream	**200 gm**

METHOD

- In a blender, add flour, butter, sugar, thyme and orange rind. Blend till the flour is crumbly. Take it out in a bowl. Add chilled water to the mix and knead into a dough. Allow to rest for 30 minutes in a fridge, wrapped in a damp cloth or a plastic film.

- Roll out thin circular discs using dry flour if required. Cut 5" diameter using a cutter. Place this dough inside the mould, push and press gently on the edges and the bottom so that the dough fits the mould. Repeat with the other mould.

- Using a fork, poke the dough on the bottom and sides. Refrigerate the moulds for 30 minutes. Remove and bake in an oven at 180 degrees for 25 minutes or till the short crust pastries are crisp and light brown. Remove and allow the moulds to cool down. Remove the shells from the moulds.

- For the orange chutney, in a bowl, add orange, sugar, cinnamon, salt and chilli powder. Add water and cook for 25 minutes, covered. Remove from heat and take out the cinnamon stick.

- Purée all the contents, including the rind but remove the seeds (if any). Pour the mix on a pan and cook on low flame till it thickens. Keep the orange chutney aside.

- In a separate bowl, add chocolate pieces. Keep aside.

- In a separate pan, add cream and bring to a boil. Pour the cream over the chocolate pieces, cover and allow the chocolate to melt. After 5 minutes, whisk the mix for a smooth consistency of a ganache.

- Fill one half of the tart (moulds) with the orange chutney and the other half with a dollop of the prepared ganache.

- Serve at room temperature or cold.

Meal 11

serves

Tomato & Avocado Shots

•

Salmon Tartare with Mango & Roasted Cumin

•

Broccolini with Toasted Almonds & Masala Polenta

•

Mishti Doi with Sesame Crisps

Tomato & Avocado Shots

INGREDIENTS

Tomato	**2 nos.** (large) (quartered & deseeded)
Tomato juice	**300 ml**
Red bell pepper	**1 no.** (small) (roughly chopped)
Basil	**2 sprigs**
Garlic	**1 clove**
Sugar	**2 tsp**
Salt	**to taste**
Pepper powder	**a generous pinch**
Avocado	**1 no.** (small) (peeled & deseeded)
Celery stalk	**1 no.** (small)
Spring onion	**1/4 cup** (chopped)
Yoghurt	**1/4 cup**
Lemon	**1 no.**

METHOD

- In a blender, add tomatoes, tomato juice, red bell pepper, basil, 1/2 garlic clove, sugar, salt and pepper powder. Blend the ingredients into a fine purée. Pour this mix into small glasses till 3/4th.

- In a separate clean blender, add the pulp of the avocados, celery, spring onions, yoghurt, salt, pepper, lemon and the remaining 1/2 garlic clove. Blend all the ingredients till the mix is smooth and runny. Using a spoon, gently top up the glasses.

- Serve chilled.

Salmon Tartare with Mango & Roasted Cumin

INGREDIENTS

Onion	**1/2 no.** (small) (finely chopped)
Green chilli	**1 no.**
Coriander	**few sprigs**
Lemon	**1 no.**
Virgin olive oil	**2 tbsp**
Salmon	**200 gm** (smoked & chopped into bite-size pieces)
Mango	**1 no.** (medium) (peeled & finely chopped)
Ginger	**1 small knob** (peeled & finely grated)
Cumin	**2 tsp** (roasted)
Salt	**to taste**
Black salt	**a pinch**

METHOD

- In a bowl, add onions, green chilli and coriander.

- Squeeze a 1/2 lemon, add 1 tablespoon olive oil, salmon and toss the mix.

- In a separate bowl, add mango and grated ginger.

- Squeeze the remaining 1/2 lemon, add cumin, salt, black salt and the remaining olive oil.

- On a plate, using a ring mould, place the mangoes first and keep the salmon on top of the mangoes.

- Remove the moulds and serve chilled.

Broccolini with Toasted Almonds & Masala Polenta

INGREDIENTS

Butter	**3 tbsp**
Cumin	**2 tsp**
Onion	**1 no.** (small) (roughly chopped)
Garlic	**2 cloves** (roughly chopped)
Green chilli	**1/2 no.** (roughly chopped)
Red bell pepper	**1 no. small** (finely chopped)
Turmeric	**1/2 tsp**
Red chilli powder	**1/2 tsp**
Polenta (instant)	**1/2 cup**
Water or stock	**2½ cups**
Salt	**to taste**
Almonds	**1/4 cup**
Broccolini	**4 stalks** (blanched & dipped in ice water)
Pepper	**to taste**

METHOD

- In a preheated pan, add 2 tablespoons of butter. Add cumin and cook for a few seconds. Add onion, garlic and green chilli. Sauté for a minute.

- Add red bell pepper to the above mix and toss well.

- Add turmeric and red chilli powder. Sauté for a few seconds and immediately add polenta. Mix well and cook for another 2 minutes.

- Add water, salt and cook on medium flame till the mix achieves porridge-like consistency.

- Wrap the almonds with a cloth and using a rolling pin, crush them.

- In a separate preheated pan, melt the remaining butter and add the crushed almonds. On slow heat, cook till the almonds turn light brown. Remove the almonds carefully and let the remaining butter stay in the pan.

- Add broccolini and toss with salt and pepper.

- Put the broccolini on a plate and pour the hot polenta on one side.

- Garnish with browned almonds.

Mishti Doi with Sesame Crisps

INGREDIENTS

Milk (full-cream)	**1 litre**
Sugar	**125 gm**
Yoghurt	**1/4 cup**
Filo sheet (12"x12")	**2 nos.**
Butter (salted)	**for basting**
Black sesame seeds	**1 tbsp**
White sesame seeds	**1 tbsp**

METHOD

- In a large pot, add milk and bring to a boil. Allow it to simmer. Keep stirring the milk till it reduces to almost half.

- In another pan, add sugar and heat it. Allow it to caramelise till the sugar achieves an amber colour. Remove from heat and pour over the hot milk and stir. Now, allow the milk to cool down till lukewarm.

- At this stage, add yoghurt to the milk and pour the mix into 2 small containers. Cover and leave untouched for about 3 hours.

- Put the yoghurt in the fridge and serve chilled.

- For the sesame crisps, place the sheets on the table and cut in half in breadth. Keep aside all the sheets except one.

- Now, baste this sheet lightly with melted butter. Sprinkle sesame seeds and gently place another sheet on top. Baste this sheet too, sprinkle more sesame seeds and place another sheet. Repeat the process.

- Now, cut the sheet into 6"x2" long strips and place in an oven tray. Bake at 170 degrees till crisp.

- Serve the crisps with mishti doi.

Meal 12

serves

Camomile & Jasmine Iced Tea

·

Burnt Eggplant Dip with Namak Para

·

Spiced Chicken & Leeks with Cucumber Dip

·

Caramelised Onion Parantha

·

Tender Coconut Pudding

Camomile & Jasmine Iced Tea

INGREDIENTS

Water	1½ cups
Sugar	2 tbsp
Fresh jasmine flower	5 nos.
Camomile teabag	6 nos.
Ice cubes	few
Mint leaves	few sprigs
Lemon juice	2 tbsp
Apple juice (sweetened)	300 ml

METHOD

- In a pan, add water and sugar. Bring to a boil. Remove from heat.

- Add jasmine flowers and camomile teabags. Allow to brew for 5 minutes.

- Take 2 tall glasses and add 4 ice cubes in each.

- In a cocktail shaker, add mint leaves and gently crush the leaves. Add lemon juice.

- Once the camomile brew cools down, add it to the cocktail shaker. Mix well.

- Pour the tea into the tall glasses with ice cubes and top up with apple juice.

- Serve immediately.

Burnt Eggplant Dip with Namak Para

INGREDIENTS

FOR THE EGGPLANT DIP

Eggplant (round)	**1 no.** (large)
Tomato	**1 no.** (medium)
Onion	**1 no.** (medium)
Potato	**1 no.** (small) (boiled & finely diced)
Green chilli	**1 no.** (chopped)
Fresh coriander	**few sprigs** (chopped)
Salt	**to taste**
Lemon	**1 no.**
Mustard oil	**2 tbsp**

FOR THE BAKED NAMAK PARA

Refined flour	**3 cups**
Salt	**1/2 tsp**
Olive oil	**3 tbsp**
Carom seeds (*ajwain*)	**2 tsp**
Water	**as required**

METHOD

- Switch on the gas stove and place the eggplant on it, over low flame. Flip the eggplant to roast both sides evenly, till the outer skin burns off. Alternatively, heat the oven to 220 degrees and roast the eggplant till the skin is charred. Remove and place on a tray and allow to cool down completely. Peel off the skin and using a large knife, mash the eggplant.

- Using a fork, prick the tomato and hover over the open flame to char its skin. Remove and place on a tray. Once cooled, remove the skin of the tomato. Repeat the process with the onion to remove its outer skin. Roughly chop the tomato and the onion.

- In a separate bowl, add eggplant, tomato, onion, potato, green chilli and coriander.

- Add salt, lemon juice and mustard oil. Mix well and refrigerate till the dip is chilled.

- For the baked namak para, mix all the ingredients along with sufficient water to make a stiff dough. Let the dough rest for 15 minutes. Roll and spread it out. Place the thin, rolled dough on a baking tray. Bake at 180 degrees for 18-20 minutes or till it becomes golden brown. Remove and allow to cool down.

- Break into smaller pieces and serve the crispy namak para with the chilled eggplant dip.

Spiced Chicken & Leeks with Cucumber Dip

INGREDIENTS

FOR THE DRY MASALA

Pomegranate seed powder	**1 tbsp**
Dry mango powder (*amchur*)	**1 tbsp**
Garam masala powder	**1 tsp**
Coriander powder	**1 tbsp**
Cumin powder	**2 tsp**
Black salt	**1 tsp**
Chilli powder	**1 tsp**

FOR THE CUCUMBER DIP

Cucumber	**1 no.** (peeled & grated)
Salt	**to taste**
Curd (thick)	**1 cup**
Coriander leaves	**few sprigs** (finely chopped)
Garlic	**1/2 clove** (minced)
Pepper	**to taste**

FOR THE SPICED CHICKEN

Gram flour	**2 tbsp**
Chicken leg	**400 gm** (boneless)
Salt	**to taste**
Lemon	**2 nos.**
Ginger paste	**1 tbsp**
Garlic paste	**1 tbsp**
Mustard oil	**3 tbsp**
Hung curd	**1/2 cup**
Leek	**1 stalk**
Oil	**2 tbsp**
Wooden skewers	**few** (submerged in water for 30 minutes)

METHOD

- For the dry masala, mix all the listed ingredients and keep aside.

- For the spiced chicken, heat a pan and add gram flour. On low heat, dry cook the gram flour till it turns blonde in colour. Remove and keep aside.

- Cut the chicken into 1.5"x1.5" cubes. Marinate the chicken with salt, lemon juice, ginger and garlic pastes.

- In a separate bowl, pour mustard oil and add dry masala mix. Mix well and add hung curd and the previously prepared roasted gram flour to this mix. Check for salt and add accordingly.

- Add this mix to the chicken and marinate well.

- Cut the leeks 2" long and add to the chicken.

- Heat a griddle and drizzle oil. Skewer the chicken and the leeks. Cook till both sides are done. Remove and serve hot.

- For the cucumber dip, in a bowl, add cucumber and a pinch of salt. Keep aside for 5 minutes.

- Squeeze out the excess water from the cucumber and add the grated cucumber to the curd along with coriander, garlic, salt and pepper.

- Stir and serve cold with the hot skewers.

Caramelised Onion Parantha

INGREDIENTS

For the Caramelised Onion

Oil	**1 tbsp**
Butter	**1 tbsp**
Onion	**2 nos.** (large) (peeled & roughly sliced)
Balsamic vinegar	**1/2 cup**
Salt	**1/2 tsp**
Pepper	**1/2 tsp**

For the Dough

Refined flour	**2½ cups**
Salt	**1/2 tsp**
Oil	**1/2 cup**
Water	**3/4 cup**
Fresh coriander	**few sprigs** (chopped) (for garnish)
Nigella Seeds (*kalonji*)	**2 tsp** (for garnish)

METHOD

- Heat a pan and add oil and butter.

- Add onions and cook on low heat for 10 minutes.

- Add balsamic vinegar, salt and pepper. Cook on low flame, covered, till the vinegar dries up. Remove and allow the mix to cool down.

- For the dough, mix 2 cups of refined flour, salt and 3 tablespoons of oil. Add water and knead into a soft dough. Let the dough rest for 15 minutes.

- Divide the dough into 4 equal-sized balls and keep aside for 5 minutes.

- Stuff each dough ball with the previously prepared caramelised onions. Using the remaining dry flour, make a disc using a rolling pin about 1/2 cm thick. Sprinkle a little water on top along with chopped coriander and nigella seeds. Press gently.

- Heat another pan and cook the parantha till both sides are evenly done.

- Use the remaining oil and cook to make the paranthas crisp.

- Remove and serve hot.

Tender Coconut Pudding

INGREDIENTS

Chia seeds	2 tbsp
Water	1 cup
Coconut milk	1½ cups
Condensed milk	1/3 cup
Apple	1/2 no. (chopped)
Strawberry	4 nos. (chopped)
Grapes	handful (chopped)
Tender coconut meat (*malai*)	4 tbsp (roughly chopped)
Mint leaves	for garnish

METHOD

- Soak the chia seeds in water for 45 minutes so that they bloom.

- In a bowl, add coconut milk and condensed milk. Whisk well.

- Add chia seeds, chopped fruits and tender coconut meat. Mix well.

- Serve chilled, garnished with mint leaves.

Meal 13

serves 2

Pineapple & Lemongrass Mojito

•

Ham & Cheese Bread Pakora

•

Chicken Seekh Masala

•

Badami Parantha

•

Desi Bread & Butter Pudding

Pineapple & Lemongrass Mojito

INGREDIENTS

Pineapple	**1 no.** (small) (peeled & cut into small pieces)
Rosemary	**2 sprigs**
Sugar	**3 tbsp**
Lemon	**1 no.**
Mint leaves	**2 sprigs**
Salt	**a pinch**
Ice cube	**8 nos.**
Lemongrass	**2 bulbs**
Carbonated water	**300 ml** (chilled)

METHOD

- In a blender, add pineapple pieces. Add rosemary, sugar, lemon juice, mint leaves, salt and ice cubes. Blend the mix well.

- Smash the lemongrass bulbs with a rolling pin and drop into a glass.

- Pour the drink in two glasses and top up with carbonated water.

- Serve.

Ham & Cheese Bread Pakora

INGREDIENTS

Bread	**4 slices**
Cheese	**4 slices**
Ham	**4 slices**
Gram flour	**2 cups**
Salt	**to taste**
Carom seeds (*ajwain*)	**2 tsp**
Chilli powder	**1 tsp**
Water	**2/3 cup**
Oil	**for grilling**

METHOD

- On a chopping board, place 2 bread slices. Add a slice of cheese followed by 2 slices of ham and add another layer of cheese on the bread slice. Cover with another slice of bread. Press gently. Repeat with the remaining bread slices.

- In a separate bowl, add gram flour, salt, carom seeds and chilli powder. Add water and whisk to make a thick batter.

- Heat a pan and lightly grease it with oil.

- Carefully dip the bread pakora in the prepared batter and coat evenly.

- In the preheated pan, cook the bread pakora for 2-3 minutes.

- Drizzle oil on top and flip the pakora. Cook for another 2-3 minutes.

- Using tongs, hold the bread pakoras and cook all the sides to ensure the batter is fully cooked.

- Remove and serve hot.

Chicken Seekh Masala

INGREDIENTS

FOR THE CHICKEN SEEKH KEBAB

Chicken	400 gm (minced)
Ginger	a knob (finely chopped)
Garlic	6 cloves (finely chopped)
Green chilli	1 no. (finely chopped)
Mint leaves	handful (finely chopped)
Fresh coriander	few sprigs (finely chopped)
Salt	to taste
Cumin seeds	2 tsp
Chilli powder	2 tsp
Soft cheese	50 gm (small piece)
Oil	3 tbsp

FOR THE MASALA

Oil	1/4 cup
Cumin	2 tsp
Onion	1 cup (chopped)
Ginger paste	2 tbsp
Garlic paste	2 tbsp
Water	as required
Turmeric	1/2 tsp
Chilli powder	1 tsp
Coriander powder	1 tbsp
Tomato	2 cups (chopped)
Salt	to taste
Green chilli	1 no. (slit)
Dried fenugreek leaves (*kasoori methi*)	1/2 tsp
Cream	1/4 cup

METHOD

- For the seekh kebab, in a bowl, add chicken mince, ginger, garlic, green chilli, mint and coriander leaves along with salt, cumin, chilli powder, cheese and oil. Mix well.

- Wet your hands with water and divide the minced chicken into 8 balls. Lightly roll the seekh kebab balls into 2" long cylindrical shapes.

- Heat a pan, grease the pan lightly with oil and cook the kebabs for 4-5 minutes on medium heat. Remove and keep aside.

- For the masala, heat oil and add cumin.

- Add onions and cook till they turn light brown.

- Add ginger-garlic paste along with little water. Cook for 2 minutes. Sprinkle turmeric, chilli powder and coriander powder and cook for another 3 minutes.

- Add tomatoes and salt. Cook for another 15 minutes on slow flame or till the oil surfaces. Add a cup of water and allow the mix to come to a boil.

- Gently drop the seekh kebabs along with green chilli into the boiling mix. Cook till the masala thickens.

- Garnish with kasoori methi and cream.

- Remove and serve hot.

Badami Parantha

INGREDIENTS

Almonds	1 cup
Water	as required
Milk	3/4 cups (approx.)
Refined flour	2½ cups
Semolina	2 tbsp
Salt	a generous pinch
Sugar	1 tbsp
Cardamom powder	1/2 tsp
Screw pine flower water (kewra)	1 tsp
Ghee	1/2 cup

METHOD

- Boil almonds in water to loosen the skin. Remove from water and allow to cool down. Peel the almonds once softened.

- In a blender, add almonds with 1/2 cup of milk. Blend to make a purée. Keep aside.

- In a bowl, add 2 cups refined flour, semolina, salt, sugar, cardamom powder, kewra, previously prepared almond purée and 1/4 cup ghee. Mix gently. Add the remaining milk to make a soft dough. Knead well and keep aside for 20 minutes, covered.

- Divide the dough into 4 equal-sized balls. Let these rest for 5 minutes. Roll out thin, circular paranthas.

- Drizzle the paranthas with ghee and lightly dust with the remaining flour.

- Start folding the parantha to make pleats. Once the pleats are done, start rolling the dough from one end in a circular motion, giving it an overlapped coil-like shape. Repeat with the remaining dough. Allow the paranthas to rest for 10 minutes.

- Roll out the dough flat, keeping the parantha about 4 mm thick.

- Heat a pan or tawa and cook the parantha. Flip the parantha after 2 minutes. Apply ghee and cook on both sides. Once done, remove and gently crush the parantha with your hands to reveal the layers of the parantha.

- Serve hot.

Desi Bread & Butter Pudding

INGREDIENTS

Milk (full fat)	**500 ml**
Sugar	**1/3 cup**
Saffron	**few strands**
Cardamom powder	**1/2 tsp**
Screw pine flower water (*kewra*)	**1 tbsp**
Fennel seeds (*saunf*)	**1 tbsp**
Black pepper powder	**a pinch**
Egg	**4 nos.** (beaten)
White bread	**8 thin slices** (sides removed)
Butter	**1/4 cup** (melted)
Pistachios	**handful**
Raisins	**handful**
Water	**as required**

METHOD

- In a pan, add milk with sugar, saffron, cardamom powder, kewra, fennel seeds and black pepper powder.

- Bring the milk to a quick boil and remove from heat. Allow the mix to cool down till it is lukewarm.

- Add eggs to the milk and whisk.

- Arrange the bread slices in a large baking mould and pour the melted butter on top.

- Add pistachios, raisins and pour the milk. Place the mould in a deep tray and fill with water till it is 3/4th of the height of the mould.

- In a preheated oven, bake at 180 degrees for 25-30 minutes.

- To check if the pudding is done, slide a knife into the centre of the pudding, if it comes out clean, it means the pudding is baked.

- Remove and serve warm or cooled.

NOTES

You can use a metal baking mould or a glass baking dish for this recipe.

Meal 14

serves

Cucumber & Lemon Colada

Masala Papad Bruschetta

Lamb with Apricots

Ghee Pulao

Masala Brownie

Cucumber & Lemon Colada

INGREDIENTS

Lemon	**3 nos.**
Sugar	**3 tbsp**
Cucumber	**1 no.** (small) (roughly chopped)
Mint leaves	**handful**
Ice cube	**6 nos.**
Carbonated water (soda)	**300 ml**

METHOD

- In a blender, squeeze the lemons and add sugar. Add cucumber, mint leaves and ice cubes. Blend well till the sugar is completely dissolved.

- Pour the drink into tall glasses and top up with soda.

- Serve chilled.

Masala Papad Bruschetta

INGREDIENTS

Onion	**2 nos.** (small) (peeled & roughly diced)
Tomato	**2 nos.** (medium) (peeled & roughly diced)
Green chilli	**1 no.** (roughly chopped)
Fresh coriander	**handful** (roughly chopped)
Peanuts	**1/4 cup** (roasted)
Salt	**to taste**
Chaat masala	**2 tsp**
Lemon	**1 no.**
Papad	**4 nos.**
Butter	**2 tbsp**
French bread	**4 slices**

METHOD

- In a bowl, add onions, tomatoes, green chilli, fresh coriander and peanuts. Mix well.

- Add salt, chaat masala and squeeze in lemon.

- In a preheated pan, dry roast the papad on both sides. Remove and allow to cool down.

- Heat a separate pan. Smear butter on the bread slices and cook to toast well.

- Remove and take a spoonful of the onion-tomato mixture and apply on the bread slices. Place these on a tray and using your hands, crush the papad and sprinkle on the toasted bread (bruschetta).

- Serve warm or cooled.

Lamb with Apricots

INGREDIENTS

Lamb chunks	**350 gm**
Salt	**to taste**
Ginger-garlic paste	**2 tbsp**
Oil	**5 tbsp**
Green cardamom	**3-4 nos.**
Black peppercorn	**5-6 nos.**
Clove	**2-3 nos.**
Cinnamon	**1 stick**
Cumin	**1 tsp**
Onion	**1 cup** (chopped)
Turmeric	**1/2 tsp**
Kashmiri chilli powder	**1 tbsp**
Coriander powder	**1 tbsp**
Cumin powder	**2 tsp**
Water	**as required**
Tomato	**1 cup** (chopped)
Jaggery	**3 tbsp** (grated)
Malt vinegar	**1/4 cup**
Apricot (dried)	**1 cup**
Coriander leaves	**few sprigs**

NOTE
The final consistency of the dish has to be thick, with the semi-dry masala coating the meat evenly.

METHOD

- Marinate the lamb chunks with salt and ginger-garlic paste. Keep aside.

- In a deep pan, heat oil. Add green cardamoms, black peppercorns, cloves, cinnamon and cumin. Cook for a few seconds and add onions. Cook on low heat till the onions turn brown.

- Add turmeric, chilli powder, coriander powder and cumin powder. Add a little water immediately and cook for another few seconds.

- Add the marinated meat to the above semi-dry masala mix and cook on high heat for 10 minutes.

- Add a cup of water, lower the heat and cook till the meat is 3/4th done. Keep adding water as and when required so that the meat does not burn.

- Add tomatoes and cook till they become soft and pulpy.

- Add jaggery and malt vinegar. Stir and cook for 2-3 minutes.

- Drop the apricots into the meat curry. Lower the heat and cook for another 10 minutes. Turn off the heat and remove.

- Garnish with fresh coriander leaves and serve.

Ghee Pulao

INGREDIENTS

Ghee	**4 tbsp**
Cumin seeds	**2 tsp**
Onion	**1 no.** (small) (peeled & roughly sliced)
Water	**2 cups**
Salt	**to taste**
Basmati rice	**1 cup** (washed & soaked for 45 minutes)
Fresh coriander	**handful** (roughly chopped)

METHOD

- Heat a deep pan and add ghee. Once hot, add cumin seeds. Stir for a few seconds and add onion slices. Cook till the onion slices turn brown.

- Add water and bring the mixture to a boil. Add salt and rice. Taste the water to check for salt. Make sure it is salty enough as the rice will absorb excess salt. Bring to a boil and cook on high heat till the water and the rice reach the same level.

- At this stage, lower the heat and cook, covered, till all the water is absorbed and the rice swells up.

- Remove, garnish with fresh coriander and serve hot.

Masala Brownie

INGREDIENTS

Water	as required
Butter	125 gm
Dark chocolate	100 gm
Egg	2 nos.
Sugar	130 gm
Flour	35 gm
Cocoa powder	40 gm
Baking powder	½ tsp
Cardamom powder	½ tsp
Fennel seeds powder (*saunf*)	½ tsp
Cinnamon powder	½ tsp
Nutmeg powder	a pinch
Walnuts	100 gm
Butter paper	½

METHOD

- In a deep pan, add water and bring to a boil. Allow it to simmer.

- In a separate bowl, add butter and dark chocolate. Mix well.

- Place the bowl on the pan. Make sure the bowl does not touch the water but heats up with the steam rising from the simmering water. Mix till the chocolate melts. Remove and keep aside.

- In another bowl, add eggs and sugar. Whisk lightly. Add flour, cocoa powder and baking powder. Mix well.

- Add dry spices to the flour mixture and mix well.

- Add the previously prepared molten chocolate, and walnuts to the mix. Mix well to achieve a smooth consistency.

- Prepare a baking tray 10"x10". Line the base and sides of the baking tray with a butter paper. Pour the mixture into the tray and spread evenly. Bake for 30 minutes at 180 degrees. Remove and allow it to cool down.

- Refrigerate for 2 hours and cut the brownie into squares.

- Serve.

Meal 15

serves

Butternut Squash & Apricot Shorba

•

Mushroom Kurkuri

•

Prawns in Coconut Milk

•

Curry Leaf Pulao

•

Peaches with Brandy & Ice Cream

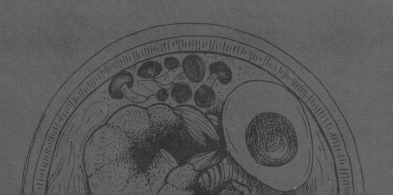

Butternut Squash & Apricot Shorba

INGREDIENTS

Butter	**3 tbsp**
Bay leaf	**1 no.**
Fennel seeds (*saunf*)	**2 tsp**
Onion	**1 no.** (small) (roughly chopped)
Celery	**1 stick** (roughly chopped)
Garlic	**5 cloves** (roughly chopped)
Ginger	**a knob** (roughly chopped)
Green chilli	**1 no.** (roughly chopped)
Butternut squash	**1 no.** (small) (peeled & roughly diced)
Apricot (dried)	**1 cup**
Turmeric	**a pinch**
Water	**5 cups**
Salt	**to taste**
Pepper powder	**to taste**
Pumpkin seeds	**handful** (lightly toasted)

METHOD

- Heat a deep vessel and melt butter.

- Add bay leaf and fennel seeds. Sauté and add onion, celery, garlic, ginger and green chilli. Sauté for 3-4 minutes on medium heat.

- Add butternut squash, apricots and turmeric. Cook for another 3 minutes.

- Add water and bring the mix to a boil. Lower the heat, cover and cook till the butternut squash is soft. Remove from heat and allow it to cool down.

- Once cooled, add it to a blender and make into a smooth purée.

- Remove the purée into a pan, add 2 cups of water and bring the mix to a boil. Simmer for 2-3 minutes, add salt pepper powder. Remove.

- Serve the butternut squash hot, garnished with toasted pumpkin seeds.

Mushroom Kurkuri

INGREDIENTS

Butter	**1 tbsp**
Cumin	**1 tsp**
Onion	**1 no.** (small) (finely chopped)
Garlic	**2-3 cloves** (finely chopped)
Green chilli	**1 no.** (finely chopped)
Button mushroom	**3 cups** (finely chopped)
Salt	**to taste**
Pepper	**to taste**
Parsley	**handful** (finely chopped)
Cheddar cheese	**120 gm** (grated)
Spring roll sheet ("6"x6")	**6 nos.**
Water	**as required**
Oil	**for deep frying**

METHOD

- Heat a pan and add butter and cumin. Cook for a few seconds.

- Add onion, garlic and green chilli. Allow these ingredients to sweat on low heat.

- Add mushrooms and cook on high flame till the moisture evaporates. Sprinkle salt and pepper. Remove and allow the mushroom mix to cool down.

- Add parsley and cheese. Mix well.

- Using a knife, divide the spring roll sheet diagonally to get 2 equal-sized triangles. Keeping the broader side of the sheet toward yourself, place a spoonful of the mixture in the centre. Moisten the sides of the sheet with a little water and fold the edges inward.

- Roll the sheet from the broader side to the narrower side. Give it the shape of a spring roll/cigar.

- In a deep vessel, heat oil and fry the rolls till crisp.

- Serve hot.

Prawns in Coconut Milk

INGREDIENTS

Butter	**2 tbsp**
Garlic	**5 cloves** (finely chopped)
Ginger	**a knob** (finely chopped)
Onion	**1 no.** (small) (finely chopped)
Green chilli	**1 no.** (slit)
Tomato	**2 nos.** (small) (diced)
White wine	**200 ml**
Coconut milk (thick)	**400 ml**
Water	**as required**
Salt	**to taste**
Pepper	**to taste**
Prawn	**12 nos.** (small) (shell-off, de-veined)
Curry leaves	**2 sprigs**
Rice flour	**2 tsp**
Coriander leaves	**handful** (roughly chopped)

METHOD

- Heat a deep vessel and melt butter.

- Add garlic, ginger and onion. Cook for 3 minutes on low flame.

- Add green chilli and stir. Add tomatoes and give a quick stir for a minute.

- On high flame, add white wine. Stir till the wine evaporates.

- Lower the heat and pour coconut milk. Add a dash of water to make the sauce thinner. Stir and season with salt and pepper.

- Bring the mix to a boil and drop in the prawns along with curry leaves.

- Separately, dissolve the rice flour in 2 tablespoons of water and add it to the coconut milk sauce. Give a quick stir so that the sauce thickens.

- Sprinkle coriander leaves on the simmering sauce.

- Once the prawns are cooked, remove and serve hot.

Curry Leaf Pulao

INGREDIENTS

Coconut oil	**2 tbsp**
Mustard seeds	**2 tsp**
Asafoetida powder (*hing*)	**1/2 tsp**
Curry leaves	**5 sprigs**
Green chilli	**1 no.** (slit)
Water	**2 cups**
Salt	**to taste**
Basmati rice	**2 cups** (washed & soaked for 45 minutes)

METHOD

- Heat a pan and add coconut oil.

- Add mustard seeds and once they crackle, add asafoetida powder followed by curry leaves and green chilli. Sauté and add water. Bring the mix to a boil.

- Add salt, followed by drained rice. Since the rice will absorb the salt, add a generous pinch of salt at this stage.

- Stir and remove the ladle. Bring the mix to a quick boil and lower the heat.

- Cook covered till all the water is used and the rice blooms.

- Remove from heat and fluff the rice with a fork and serve hot.

Peaches with Brandy & Ice Cream

INGREDIENTS

Butter	1 tbsp	Orange juice	1 cup
Orange	1 no. (peeled, rind segmented)	Honey	2 tbsp
		Vanilla extract	1/2 tsp
		Lemon	1 no.
Cinnamon	1 stick	Basil leaves	few sprigs + for garnish
Peach	4 nos. (medium) (cut into two, pit removed)	Vanilla ice cream	2 scoops
Brandy	80 ml		

METHOD

- Heat a pan and add butter, orange rind and cinnamon.

- On the pan, place the peaches with the skin side up and cook for 2 minutes.

- Add brandy and give the pan a gentle swirl. Once the brandy evaporates, add orange juice to the mix.

- Add honey, vanilla extract and squeeze a lemon. Cover and cook on very low flame for 2-3 minutes.

- Add basil leaves to the juice and remove from heat. Allow the cool down for 3-4 minutes.

- While still warm, carefully lift the peaches and place them in a bowl. Add a scoop of vanilla ice cream alongside the peaches and pour the juice from the pan over the peaches.

- Garnish with fresh basil leaves and serve.

Acknowledgements

I grew up in a family of food lovers. Every man in my family talks about food with an unrelenting passion and unconditional love. They take pride in whatever dish they rustle up for their loved ones. My culinary journey is therefore incomplete without the collective efforts of all the people who have been by my side through the ebbs and flows of life.

I would like to thank:

My big Punjabi family, especially my (late) grandfather, father and uncle, for being the source of inspiration and a pillar of strength;

My teachers and chef mentors at IHM Chandigarh, whose guidance shaped me and instilled in me the passion for food and the kitchen;

My extraordinary team at Food Konnect: Amit, Adil, Ganesh and Abhinay, with you around, cooking seems like a breeze;

Pratik Palande, your pictures add a different dimension to *Kunal Kapur in the Kitchen*;

Aman Choutani, your lovely cover shot adds the Midas touch;

The very hard-working team at Om Books International—publisher Ajay Mago, editor-in-chief Dipa Chaudhuri, creative head Arijit Ganguly, and editors Ipshita Mitra and Simran Kaur—for treating this book as your own;

And, to each and everyone who have, in your own way, inspired my cooking. With each passing day, I keep adding to this list. Cheers!

Index

Soup, Tempered Yoghurt Soup, 35

Spiced Chicken & Leeks with Cucumber Dip, 144

Spinach & Apricot Kofta with Pumpkin
Tomato Sauce, 110

Steamed Ginger Fish, 63

Strawberry & Ginger Sangria, 11

T

Tamarind Date Chutney, 120

Tea, Camomile & Jasmine Iced Tea, 140

Tempered Yoghurt Soup, 35

Tender Coconut Pudding, 148

Thandai Crème Brûlée, 42

Tomato & Avocado Shots, 131

Tomato & Rosemary Pulao, 17

Turnip Purée with Chilli Garlic Bread, 84

W

Wasabi Butter, 101

Watermelon, Mint & Ginger Slushie, 107